If you were me and lived in...
THE AMERICAN WEST

Carole P. Roman
Illustrated by Paula Tabor

For Kevin and Stuart - Saddle Up

Book Design by Kelsea Wierenga

Copyright © 2016 Carole P. Roman

All rights reserved.

ISBN-10: 1-947118-51-X

ISBN-13: 978-1-947118-51-5

If you were me and lived in...

THE AMERICAN WEST

This is Willamette Valley today in Oregon. It is a beautiful and lush piece of land where many people traveled from the east to settle in the 19th century.

This is the homestead your parents built in 1843 after a long and difficult journey on the Oregon Trail. A homestead is a large piece of property with a farm and other structures on the land that belong to your family.

There had been record flooding on the East coast making farming unproductive. Food and money were scarce. People needed to relocate.

You were a twelve-year-old boy when your parents left everything they knew in Ohio and decided to go find a better life and richer land with the "The Great Migration of 1843."

Migration meant movement, but you prefered to call it when you joined the "Wagon Train of 1843" because it sounded better.

Your name could have been Clarence or Ethan if you were a boy. Your parents could have picked Lucy or Minerva for your sister's name.

Your mother did not want to leave because she was afraid it might be worse in the new territories.

Your father had heard about the beautiful farmland from your uncle who went to find a better life.

Uncle Silas traveled in search for gold he heard people had discovered in a place called California. He wrote about the rich land he saw along the way that was free for the taking for farmers willing to take the risk and move there.

He didn't find gold, instead choosing to settle on a parcel of land in Oregon and urged your father to join him.

Your father sold his farm and most of his furniture, and bought a covered wagon, called a "conestoga" (con-a-stog-a) for traveling. You heard that people called it a prairie schooner (prar-ree skoo-ner) because it looked like a boat. Your father purchased two oxen for the trip. You wanted to take horses, but he said oxen will eat grass on the road; horses needed grain, which was heavy as well as costly.

Together your family headed to Independence, Missouri, to meet up with thousands of other people making the 2,000 mile journey to farm the fertile land available out west. There were teachers, carpenters, farmers, merchants, and people from all over the world. You met somebody from Ireland! He came from across the ocean.

It was early May, and your parents were advised they must travel in the summer to avoid the harsh winter. The wagon trains were put together to keep the thousands of people moving safely through the vast and unfamiliar territory.

Your mother had packed your wagon with barrels of supplies.

She took 200 pounds of flour, 150 pounds of salt pork or bacon, 20 pounds of sugar, 10 pounds of salt, 60 pounds of beans, and 25 pounds of coffee, as well as yeast, crackers, eggs, cornmeal, potatoes, rice, dried meat, dried fruit, and water to drink.

She had her sewing kit, plates, utensils, medicine, lanterns, and wax to make candles. There was no place to buy supplies on the frontier.

Your father packed all his tools. Many people brought herds of sheep and other farm animals.

You had one cow, two goats, and a pig.

You remember the five month journey as a hard experience, but it toughened you up for the frontier ahead.

You traveled in single file and knew that your group did indeed look like the cars of a train.

You had many friends; seven families from your hometown in Ohio were on the trip as well. One person was elected leader. He blew a whistle every morning, waking everybody up and getting the group moving.

You liked running beside the trail guide's horse. His name was Sam, and he was a fur trapper. He lived and traveled this area for years. He was paid to ride ahead and see what to expect the next day. He wore animal skins and had a rifle.

Your father was chosen to be on the council that helped govern the entire group and settle arguments.

You had two changes of clothing to wear on the trip. You had two pairs of canvas pants called jeans. Both you and your father had another tucked away for the homestead called overalls. They had a bib made from the canvas material over the chest area to protect your shirt when you actually started farming. You wore a cotton shirt, suspenders, and boots. Both you and your father wore a low crown hat to shield your eyes from the sun.

Your sister and mother had dresses made in bright red gingham, which is sort of a check design. The material was an inexpensive and sturdy cotton. They had tightly fitted bodices and wore petticoats (pet-tee-coat) underneath the full skirt. They both wore an apron made from white linen over it. A cotton bonnet protected their faces from the harsh sunlight. They each had a pair of boots, too.

You had to milk the cow while your sister gathered wood and buffalo chips to make a fire to cook dinner. You were glad she had to gather the buffalo chips. They were a nicer name for buffalo poop. They could smell nasty, too.

Your sister helped wash dishes, but you had to run to the local riverbeds to bring the water to your mother.

Your father taught you to help skin the animals he was able to hunt along the way, and you did enjoy the fresh turkey, rabbit, and buffalo when they were caught.

Your sister hated churning butter. She realized that if she hung a pail of milk on the wagon, all the bouncing around created butter, and she didn't have to do that boring chore.

Breakfast was hot coffee and hardtack, which is a very dry biscuit.

Lunch was usually a bowl of beans.

You walked next to the wagon between ten and twenty miles per day.

Your sister whined enough so that she was placed next to your mother who drove the wagon.

When you made camp, your mother cooked meals over an open fire in a dutch oven. That was a big, black cast iron pot and was extremely heavy.

The whole meal was made in one pot. She always had dumplings or biscuits to serve with beans and whatever meat you father was able to shoot or trap.

At night, the wagons formed a large circle for safety and you and your sister could run and play with other children. After your chores were done, that is.

You slept outside the wagon wrapped in an old quilt beside the wheel. You could count hundreds of stars in the dark night.

If you had to describe the trip in one word, it would be mud! When it rained, and it did often enough, the whole ground turned into a mess.

Wheels got stuck in the thick mud. You learned to put grass on the ground in front of the wheels and then joined all the men pushing from behind. The wheels turned on the grass, and the oxen pulled it out of the mud.

The dust was bad too. If there was no rain, it was so dry, the whole train had to stop because nobody could see through the clouds of dust. You had to cover your mouth with a bandana to protect it from the dirt and sand. Sometimes, you couldn't even see your hand, and it was right in front of your face!

You met natives along the way you called Indians.

You learned that they came from a vast number of tribes such as the Pawnee (Paw-nee), Cheyenne (Shy-ann), Comanche (Co-man-chee), Sioux (Sue), Arapaho (A-rap-oh), Shoshone (Show-show-nee), Paiute (Pie-yoot), Cayuse (Kayh-use), and Wasco (Wah-sko) to name a few. You learned that each group was varied with different languages and customs.

You heard stories about attacks and great battles but only met friendly people who wanted to exchange their products for yours. They eagerly traded blankets and pottery with the people on the wagon train.

Many settlers died during the long trip. Illness, accidents, and in rare cases, you heard of conflicts with the natives caused deaths.

Sanitation was poorly planned. There was a cholera (ka-le-ra) outbreak when you made camp beside the Platte River. Many people got the stomach ailment. It was a terrible time. Some were so sick they couldn't continue the trip; others died.

Some women decided to finish the trip alone when their husbands died.

A woman could never be a chief or even vote in the assemblies. Women were, however, respected and had more freedom than most of the women in Europe. They managed their household finances and stepped in to make marriages for their children if their husbands weren't there.

There were new marriages along the way. People realized the trip would be easier if they were a couple. Sometimes young couples met and married once they got permission from their parents.

You loved looking at the prairie grass as you walked during that long dusty summer. It swayed in the breeze like waves in the ocean. You finally understood how the wagon got its nickname of prairie schooner.

By the time you got to Oregon territory, all the men had to hack away at the dense trees to create a trail.

At the Columbia River, they had to take the wagons apart to float on the water to get to the opposite bank.

You herded the animals through the rushing river, and when you got to the other side, you said you were never going back over it again.

Crossing that river was the scariest part of the entire trip.

Once you found your new home, you were happy. Your parents were granted 640 acres of free land. All they had to do was farm it! It was on the other side of the Columbia River.

It was a flat piece of land, surrounded by three sets of mountains. It had a mild climate, and your family set up camp.

With the remaining money, your father bought wood at the mill, and you helped him build a one room cabin with a packed earth floor.

It had two windows covered in greased paper because there was no glass available.

You used daub (dawb) and chink which is mud and grass to close the gaps in the walls. You built a large fireplace that took up an entire wall. The door faced south, so you had sunlight all day. You built a small outhouse for the necessary business of life. It was mighty cold to run out there in the middle of the night, but when you had to go, you had to go!

You worked equally fast building a barn as well to protect the livestock. Some of the families pitched together, working in groups to get the work done faster. That meant you had to help them as well, delaying the preparation of the land for farming.

You settled in for the winter, reading the bible daily with your mother, and resting up for the spring planting.

You often wondered where all the Indians that you heard about lived. Soon you found out that many had died from diseases brought by the settlers. There were only a few hundred left. They lived peacefully with you as your neighbor.

Spring came quickly. You cleared the land using the oxen to drag the plow and make long furrows in the rich soil. Your father planted corn and wheat. Your mother planted a kitchen garden filled with peas, carrots, beets, spinach, and potatoes.

Everyday you milked the cow and chopped wood for the fireplace. Your sister fed the chickens and helped your mother spin wool for clothes.

Another summer passed, and you were devastated to learn that in the winter, you were expected to go to the one room schoolhouse that the families organized down the road.

You complained you had too much to do, but your mother packed both you and your sister lunch pails, and you went off to do schoolwork for six hours a day. You had a piece of chalk and a slate.

Miss Evans taught all fourteen children, and you ended up finding history interesting.

You admitted to being sad when school closed in the spring for planting and looked forward to going in the summer. It would close again in the fall in time for the harvest when you were expected to help with the farm.

Soon a small town grew nearby the schoolhouse. You had a saloon, a general store, a blacksmith, and a church you could go to on Sunday. Every few months all the families would get together and plan a dance. Your friend, Jonas, played the fiddle, and you danced a polka with a girl from school named Sally!

You longed to leave home and become a cowboy. You knew they made up to 25 dollars a month. They slept in bunkhouses with other cowboys, rode on cattle drives, and went to rodeos! Once when you went into town, you heard them singing in the saloon. They were happy and had fun instead of the backbreaking work of a farmer. They called settlers names like *tenderfoot*, *pilgrim*, and *greenhorn*. It seemed like a much more exciting life.

However, your parents needed your help, especially since your father broke his arm this past winter. You didn't go back to school due to your increased workload.

For your birthday, your parents gave you your own horse and saddle and taught you some important rules.

You learned that you never wave at another man when on a horse; you just nod. You must never take another man's horse without permission.

You must always help another person in need, always give a nice greeting by saying "Howdy," and lastly, never put on another man's hat.

So you see, if you were me, how life in the American West could really be.

Famous people from the American West

Annie Oakley (1860-1926)- an American sharpshooter who worked in various circuses and shows to display her talent. She joined Buffalo Bill's Wild West Show, traveling the world and became an international star.

Daniel Boone (1734-1820)- was an American explorer, frontiersman, and pioneer who became a great folk hero in American culture. He was a trailblazer who moved westward, creating settlements in Kentucky and easier routes for people to follow.

Geronimo (Ge-ron-ah-mo) (1829-1909)- important leader of the Apache (Uh-pach) tribe. He carried out numerous raids against the Mexican and United States military in the southwestern American territories, resulting from conflicts of land being settled by pioneers traveling west.

Lewis and Clark Expedition- also known as the Corps of Discovery and the first trip to cross into the western portion of the Unites States that began in May of 1804 near St. Louis. President Thomas Jefferson ordered it after he made the Louisiana Purchase to find out what the new territories held. Captain Meriwether Lewis and Second Lieutenant William Clark led the journey which lasted two years. They had to explore and map the new lands and find a practical route westward. They also studied the geography and animal life as well as establish trade with local tribes.

Red Cloud (1822-1909)- lead the Native American forces in the famous Red Cloud War over control of lands in northeastern Wyoming and Montana.

Sacajawea (Sa-ga-jeh-way-ya) (1788-1812)- a Native American Shoshone tribe woman who helped the Lewis and Clark expedition map and explore the Louisiana Purchase. She helped them establish contact with the many tribes in the western territories.

Wild Bill Hickok (1837-1876)- a folk character popular in the Old West. A soldier from the Civil War, he moved west, becoming famous as a stagecoach driver, scout, marksman, lawman, actor, and professional gambler.

Wyatt Earp (Wy-ett Urp) (1848-1929)- a well-known deputy sheriff in Tombstone, Arizona, involved in the famous "Gunfight at the OK Corral."

Glossary

Apache (Uh-pach)- A group of Native American people from the southwest part of the United States.

Arapaho (A-rap-oh)- a member of the North American Native Americans who spoke the Algonquian (Al-gon-kee-uhn) language.

bib (bib)- the part of a piece of clothing that covers the area above a person's waist.

blacksmith (blak-smith)- a person who creates tools and horseshoes in a forge.

bodice (bod-is)- a woman's vestlike garment similar to a corset.

bonnet (bon-net)- a hat that ties under the chin.

buffalo chips (buf-fal-o)- buffalo poop.

bunkhouse (bunk-haus)- a building in which workers sleep.

California (Cal-uh-forn-ya)- a state in the southwestern area of the United States on the Pacific coast.

Cayuse (Kayh-use)- a North American tribe of Native Americans who settled in Oregon.

Cheyenne (Shy-ann)- a group of Native Americans who once lived between the Missouri and Arkansas rivers. They settled in Montana and Oklahoma on reservations.

chink (cha-ink)- a small cleft, slit, or fissure between two boards of wood.

cholera (ka-le-ra)- any of several diseases of humans and domestic animals, usually marked by severe stomach problems.

Clarence (Clar-ance)- a popular boy's name in the American West.

Columbia River (Kuh-lum-bee-ia River)- a river that flows through the southwest parts of the Canada and northwest parts of the United States and into the Pacific Ocean.

Comanche (Co-man-chee)- the Shoshonean tribe located in the southwestern part of the United States and live entirely on the Great Plains.

conestoga (con-a-stog-a)- a wagon with large wheels used to transport pioneers and freight.

cowboy (cow-boi)- a man who rides a horse and takes care of cows or horses in the Western United States.

daub (dawb)- plaster, clay, or another substance used for coating a surface, especially when mixed with straw to form a wall.

dumplings (dum-plings)- a boiled ball of dough used in stews or soups.

dutch oven (dutch-ov-en)- a large covered pot.

Ethan (E-than)- popular boy's name in the American West.

expedition (ex-pe-dit-shun)- a group of people who travel together to a distant place.

fiddle (fid-del)- violin.

furrows (fur-rows)- a long and narrow cut in the ground.

fur trapper (fur trap-per)- a person who hunts animals and sells the hides and fur for profit.

greenhorn (green-horn)- a person who doesn't have much experience and knowledge.

general store (gen-er-al)- a store usually in a small town that sells many different things including groceries.

gingham (ging-ham)- a cotton cloth that often is marked with a pattern of colored squares.

Gold Rush (Goal-dah Rush)- a situation in which many people go quickly to a place where gold has been discovered because they hope to find more gold and become rich.

hardtack (hard-tak)- a saltless hard biscuit, bread, or cracker.

homestead (hom-sted)- a family's land including the house and outbuildings.

"Howdy!" (Hau-dee)- used as an informal greeting.

Indians (In-dee-ans)- the name by which the settlers called the different tribes of Native Americans.

Jonas (Jo-nas)- popular boy's name in the American West.

linen (lin-en)- a smooth, strong cloth made from flax.

Louisiana Purchase (Loo-ee-zee-ann-uh Pur-chas)- (1803) was a land deal between the United States and France, when United States bought about 827,000 square miles of land west of the Mississippi River for $15 million.

Lucy (Lou-cee)- popular girl's name in the American West.

marksmen (marks-man)- a person skilled in shooting at a mark or target.

migration (my-gray-shun)- the move from one country, place, or locality to another.

Minerva (Min-erv-a)- popular girl's name in the American West.

Ohio (Oh-hi-oh)- Northwest state located in the middle of the United States.

Oregon Territory (Or-uh-gon Terr-uh-tor-ee)- also known as the Treaty of 1846, where the United States and Great Britain claimed land.

outhouse (out-haus)- a small outdoor building that is used as a toilet.

overalls (ov-er-alls)- pants with a bib to protect the shirt.

Paiute (Pie-yoot)- a group of Native Americans of the Uto-Aztecan family.

Pawnee (Paw-nee)- Native Americans from North America Plains who mostly settled by the Platte River valley.

petticoat (pet-tee-coat)- a skirt that a woman or girl wears under a dress or outer skirt.

pilgrim (pil-grim)- a term to make fun of an early settler without experience.

pioneer (pi-on-neer)- someone who is one of the first people to move to and live in a new area.

Platte River (Plat River)- a huge river that flows in the Nebraskan state.

plow (plau)- a piece of farm equipment that is used to dig into and turn over soil, especially to prepare the soil for planting.

polka (pol-ka)- a lively dance for couples.

prairie (prar-ree)- a large, mostly flat area of land in North America that has few trees and is covered in grasses.

prairie schooner (prar-ree skoo-ner)- the name for the wagons used on the wagon train because they looked like ships sailing on the water.

relocate (re-lo-cait)- to move to another place.

rodeos (ro-day-os)- an event in which people compete at riding horses and bulls and catching animals with ropes.

Sally (Sal-lee)- a popular girl's name in the American West.

saloon (sa-loon)- a place where alcoholic drinks are served.

sanitation (san-i-tat-shun)- the promotion of hygiene and prevention of disease by maintenance of sanitary conditions.

scout (scout)- a person who explores in order to obtain information.

settlers (set-lers)- those who move and make a home in a new place.

sharpshooter (sharp-shoo-ters)- a person who is a good shot with a rifle.

Shoshone (Show-show-nee)- a Native American tribe that settled mostly in Idaho, Wyoming, and Nevada.

slate (sla-te)- a small sheet of slate in a wooden frame that was used in schools in the past for writing on with chalk.

Silas (Sy-las)- a popular boy's name in the American West.

Sioux (Sue)- a Native American tribe that lived and settled in the northern Great Plains, Minnesota, eastern Montana, and Nebraska.

tenderfoot (ten-der-fut)- a person who is not used to living in rough conditions or outdoors.

territory (te-rit-tor-ree)- one of the parts of the United States that is not a state.

trail guide (trale-guide)- a scout who leads the wagon train because he knows the route.

Wasco (Wah-sko)- Native Americans from northern Oregon.

Wyoming (Why-oh-ming)- a state located in the northwestern part of the United States.

www.ingramcontent.com/pod-product-compliance
Lightning Source LLC
Chambersburg PA
CBHW050756110526
44588CB00002B/18